SPORTS & MUSIC

LUCIUS SHEPARD

This deluxe chapbook is limited to 1000 signed & numbered copies of which this is number 617.

ARTWORK BY ARNIE FENNER

sports
&
music

SPORTS AND MUSIC

LUCIUS SHEPARD

MARK V. ZIESING BOOKS
SHINGLETOWN, CA 1994

ZIESING CHAPBOOK #1

Mark V. Ziesing
P.O. Box 76
Shingletown, CA 96088

Interior design by Robert Frazier

Printed in the United States of America
First Edition

Trade Edition
ISBN 0-929480-25-2

For two fine ladies:
Alice and Ellen

CONTENTS

sports in america

While they waited for Milchuk to show, Carnes leafed through *Sports Illustrated*, the NFL Preview issue, and Penner checked out the baseball scores in *The Globe*. They were parked on Main Street in Hyannis, across from the Copper Kitchen, where Milchuk—so they had been told—liked to have his breakfast. It was a quarter to seven of a bitter September morning, a few raindrops spitting down and ridges of leaden cloud shouldering in off the harbor. Carnes, pinch-faced and wiry, with sprays of straw-colored hair sticking out from beneath his Red Sox cap, betrayed no sign of anxiety. But Penner, who had never done this sort of work before, shifted restlessly about, flexing his neck muscles, reshaping the folds of his newspaper, and glancing this way and that.

Christ, he thought, I don't want this. He had been insane to go along with it. His mind had not been right. Too much pressure. Too much drink, too many sleepless nights. He would run, he decided, lose himself among the houses down by the ferry dock. His hand inched toward the door handle.

Carnes coughed, noisily turned the pages of his magazine, and Penner, stiffening, gave up any idea of running. He touched the pistol stuck in his belt, the envelope stuffed with bills in his windbreaker, as if acknowledging the correspondence between his salvation and another man's extinction.

To strengthen his resolve, he pictured himself returning home, with Barbara warm and sweet in their bed, hair fanned out across the pillow, her cheekbone perfection evident even in sleep. Fifty grand, he'd say to her, tossing the money onto the sheet as if it were nothing. Fifty fucking grand. And that's just for starters. Then he would show her the gun, tell her what he had done for her and how much he intended to do, maybe frighten her a little, make her understand that she might be at risk here, that the next affair might not be so readily forgiven, and that perhaps she had not chosen wrongly after all, perhaps this newly desperate, bloody-handed Penner was just the man to guarantee her summers in Newport and winters in Bermuda.

He gazed out the window, searching for favorable signs, something to restore his sense of purpose. Overhead, a pair of laced-together sneakers looped over a telephone line heeled and kicked in a stiff breeze, bringing to mind a gallows dance. The deserted sidewalks and glass storefronts with their opaque wintry reflections had the look of a stage set waiting for lights, camera, action.

"Y'see this article here 'bout the guy owns the 'Niners," Carnes said with sudden animation. "Y'know, that guy DiBartalo."

"Fuck the son of a bitch," said Penner glumly.

Carnes folded his magazine into a tube and stared at

him deadpan.
"Lighten up, willya?" he said. "Ain't no reason you gettin' nervous. The man shows...*bing!* We're outta here."

"I'm not nervous," Penner said. "I just don't feel like bullshitting seven o'clock in the morning 'bout some dumb-ass owns a football team."

"The guy's okay, man! He ain't nothin' like the other *schmucks* owns teams." And he explained how DiBartalo was in the habit of lavishing gifts upon his players. Ten thousand dollar rings, trips to Hawaii. How he sent their wives on shopping sprees at Neiman Marcus.

"Just 'cause he treats 'em like prize poodles, that makes him into Albert Schweitzer?" Penner said. "Get real!"

"I'm tellin' ya, man! Y'should read the article!"

"I don't hafta read the article, I know alla 'bout the bastard. He's a short little fucker, right? 'Bout five-five or something."

"So?" Carnes said stiffly; he stood about five-eight himself.

"So he's got a Napoleonic complex, man. His dick's on the line with the goddamn team. He could give a shit about 'em really, but 'long as they win, sure, he's gonna throw 'em a bone now and then."

Carnes muttered something and went back to reading. The silence oppressed Penner. Carnes' conversation had stopped him from thinking about Barbara. It struck him as an irony that Carnes could in any way be a comfort to him. In high school fifteen years before they had taken an instant dislike to one another. Since that time they had maintained the scantiest of relationships, this only due to the fact of their having roots in the same neighborhood, the same gang. Both men had been in the process of being groomed for positions in the Irish mob. Providing cheap muscle, running drugs. After high school Carnes had continued on this track, whereas Penner, dismayed by the bloody requisites of the life, had attended Boston College and then gotten into real estate. Yet here they were. Partnered once again by hard times and a common heritage.

"You still root for the 'Niners, huh?" he asked, and Carnes said, "Yeah," without glancing up.

"How come you root for a team like that, man? Fucking team's gotta quarterback named for a state, for Chrissakes! Joe Montana! Sounds like some kinda New York art faggot. Some guy takes pictures of dudes with umbrellas stuck up their ass."

Carnes blinked at him, more confused than angry. "Fuck you talkin?"

"Man was named for another state, I could relate," Penner went on. "Like New Jersey. I could support him maybe, he was named Joe New Jersey. Maybe he'd play a little tougher, too."

"You're fuckin' crazy!" Carnes looked alarmed, as if what Penner had said was so extreme, it might be symptomatic of dangerous behavior. "Joe Montana's the greatest quarterback in the history of the NFL."

Penner gave an amused sniff. "Yeah, he's history, all right. Sorta like the Red Sox, huh? What's it they lost now? Six in a row? Seven? The tradition continues."

Carnes glared at him. "Don't start with that shit, okay?"

Penner fingered out a pack of Camels. In school, he had delighted in mind-fucking Carnes, pushing him to the brink of rage, making the creepy little mad boy twitch, then easing up. Pushing and easing up, over and over, until Carnes was punchy from surges of adrenaline. The Red Sox, to whom he was irrationally, almost mystically devoted, had been a particular sore point.

"Course," Penner went on in a lighthearted tone, "soon as Clemens comes back, he'll make it all better. Isn't that right, man? Ol' Rocket Roger! This redneck with the IQ of a doughnut, guy doesn't have the brains to lift himself from the game when his shoulder blows up the size of a watermelon, he's gonna walk on water and win three in the Series." He shook his head in mock sympathy and lit up a Camel. "Don'tcha ever get sick of it, man?"

"I'm fuckin' sick of you, that's for sure."

"Naw, I mean doesn't it ever sink in that the guys own the Sox, they're never gonna put out the money y'need to have a winner. Alls they care 'bout is the stadium's full. Else why'd they pass up grabbin' Willie McGee off the waiver wire. See that fat fuck Gorman on TV the other night? 'Where would we play McGee?' he's saying. Right! Like where we gonna play a guy steals you fifty bases and leads the National League in hitting?"

"It's easy for you talkin' this shit!" Carnes said angrily. "You're just a frontrunner, man. You don't know how it is, you grow up with a team, you follow 'em your whole life."

"Bullshit, I'm a frontrunner!"

"Hell you ain't! Every team gets goin' good, you jump on the goddamn bandwagon. First you're a Lakers' fan. Then the A's start winnin', and..."

"I told you, man, I lived four years in Oakland."

"Big fuckin' deal! I lived in Houston, and I ain't no Astros fan."

"What'd be the point? They're even more pathetic than the Sox."

"Goddamn it! I don't hafta take this crap!" Carnes pounded a fist against the dash. "I told McDonough I couldn't work with you, man! You ain't professional! Fuckin' guy's gotta be crazy thinkin' I can spend a coupla hours in a fuckin' car with you!"

This broke Penner's mood. "Yeah, maybe," he said, remembering McDonough in the lamplit gloom of his study, his white hair agleam, patrician features seamed with anguish, noble head bowed under the weight of a daughter's dishonor. His pain, or rather Penner's sympathy with it, had glossed over the illogic of McDonough's proposal that he and Carnes become partners in a proxy vengeance. And yet afterward he'd had the thought that the scene seemed posed. Too perfect a setting, too splendid a grief. A cinematic version of Celtic woe.

"'Maybe', what?" said Carnes fiercely.

"I just can't figure it."

"What? What can't you figure?"

"Everything, man. Like why'd the man pay us so much? And in advance. He coulda hired somebody half the price. Less, even."

"He's always doin' shit like that. Remember when Bobby Doyle's kid needed a new liver. Fuckin' McDonough, he don't ask for no collection. He just digs down in his pocket. Like the man said. We help him, he helps us. We whack out the guy did his daughter, he takes care of us. That's how he's always been."

"Sure, he's a fucking saint."

"Hey, man! He's a mick's got some power in the state house and ain't forgotten where he comes from. In Southie that amounts to the same thing. You spent more time in the neighborhood steada hangin' out with those guido fucks in Back Bay, maybe you start thinkin' like an Irishman again."

"That still doesn't explain why he'd put the two of us together."

It appeared that Carnes was about to speak, but he remained silent.

"What were you gonna say?" asked Penner.

"Nothin', man!"

Penner, edging toward paranoia, could have sworn he detected the beginnings of a smirk.

A gray Lincoln Town Car came quiet as a shadow past them; it pulled into a parking space thirty feet farther along. Carnes' hand went inside his jacket. A cold, crawly trickle inched down between Penner's shoulder blades. He stubbed out his cigarette in the ash tray. His fingers looked oddly white and unreal the way they pushed and worked at the butt, like the segmented parts of some weird animal. Please God, he said to himself, unsure whether he was praying for strength or permission to chicken out.

"Just you get in back of him." Carnes's voice was tight. "I'll handle the talkin'."

They waited until Milchuk started to climb out of the Lincoln. Then they walked rapidly toward him, their breath steaming white. Milchuk was bending down into the car, fussing with papers in a briefcase. He straightened, looking puzzled. He was younger and bigger than Penner had figured. Early thirties. Six-three, six-four, maybe two-twenty. His handsome, squarish face had a rosy-cheeked pallor. His black hair and mustache were neatly trimmed, but his jaw was dirtied with stubble. He had on a very nice herringbone tweed overcoat, the kind with velvet on the lapels. Penner himself owned a similar coat, though it was several years older and far more worn. He felt a measure of resentment toward Milchuk for inadvertently showing him up.

"'Scuse me, Mister Milchuk. We have a minute of your time?" Carnes took a stand that forced Milchuk to turn his back on Penner.

Milchuk made an impatient noise and said, "I got an appointment."

When Penner poked him with his automatic, he stiffened but did not turn his head to try and see the gun as someone might who had never been that route before. Penner could feel Milchuk's pulse in his gun hand, he could feel the whole breathing mass of nerves, bones, and meat. In the chill air the man's cologne had a stinging, astringent scent.

"Awright, be cool, guys," Milchuk said. "I got a coupla hundred in my wallet. Inside pocket of the overcoat."

"How 'bout you takin' a stroll over to the car," Carnes said. "The blue Caddy back there."

"What?" said Milchuk. He snuck a peek at the car, and Penner, in a sympathetic reaction, had a peek along with him. With its vanity plates that read SOX FAN 1 and the Red Sox logo painted on the hood, the Caddy had an absurdly innocent look.

Carnes let out an exasperated sigh. "Hope you ain't gonna give us no trouble, Mister Milchuk, 'cause this is a very simple deal, what's happenin' here. Now I wantcha to get in the back seat of the Caddy with my associate there, okay? We're gonna drive you down the Cape a ways to where a man's waitin' for us. He's gonna talk to ya, tell ya a few things. Then we'll drive you back to Hyannis so's you can have your breakfast."

Milchuk darted his eyes from side to side. Searching for police cars, brave strangers. "You guys workin' for Masacola?"

"Masacola?" Carnes said. "Who's that?"

"Listen," said Milchuk, talking fast. "I dunno what this is alla 'bout, but we can work somethin' out, you guys and me."

"Either get in the fuckin' car," Carnes said flatly, "or swear to God I'm gonna knock you cold and throw ya in it. Now I'm very sincere about this, Mister Milchuk. Nothin' bad's gonna happen 'long as you don't give us no shit. Little drive in the country, little conversation. But dick us around, man, I'm gonna put lumps on your lumps. Okay?"

Milchuk drew a deep breath, blew it out. "Okay," he said, and took a step toward the Caddy.

"Hey!" Carnes pulled him back. "You gonna leave your car wide open? Your briefcase just lyin' there?" He seemed appalled by the prospect.

Milchuk glanced at Penner, as if seeking a form of validation. Penner tried to keep his face empty.

"Lock the bitch, willya?" Carnes said. "If you want, take the case with ya. You leave a fuckin' car like that unlocked, man, some nigger's gonna be ridin' it around Roxbury."

This solicitude was a beautiful touch, Penner thought. Extremely professional. He could not help admiring Carnes for it. Milchuk collected his papers, locked up the Lincoln. And as they walked to the Caddy, Penner could tell by the firmness of his step that the dead man felt much better about his future.

Ten minutes out of Hyannis, heading toward Cotuit, and the overcast started to break. There was the merest line of blue above the islands, and directly ahead, a blare of silvery sunlight in roughly the shape of a cross seamed the division between mountains of black clouds, making a dark and mysterious glory of the eastern sky. Now and then Penner saw flashes of sun-spattered water between the sparsely needled pines along the roadside. Despite the tackle shops, the clam shacks, motels and souvenir stores, there was something eerie and desolate about the Cape, a fundamental emptiness. It was a flat, scoured jumble of a land, flat rocks and flat fields, thickets and stunted trees, moors punctuated by the blue dots of glacial ponds, sloping shingles figured with capsized scallop boats, cork floats, torn fishing nets, all surrounded by the dreary flatness of the sea. Penner found it more than usually depressing.

Static burst from the radio as Carnes spun the tuning dial, settling on a talk show—some asshole with a sardonic baritone goading housewives into bleating out idiot opinions on the economy. Penner kept his gun pressed against Milchuk's side and watched him out of the corner of his eye. He halfway hoped Milchuk would try for the gun. But Milchuk sat like a man in a trance, holding the briefcase to his chest, staring straight ahead. Once he asked how far they had left to go, and Carnes, with folksy amiability, said damn if he knew, he'd never been out on the Cape before, but it couldn't be much farther.

The talk show host began discussing the Red Sox, their recent decline, and Carnes said over his shoulder, "Ever play any ball, Mister Milchuk? You look like a ballplayer to me."

Milchuk was startled. "I played in college," he said after a second.

"I thought so. What's your position? First base? Outfield?"

"Rightfield."

"So I guess you a Sox fan, huh?"

"Yeah, sure."

"Follow 'em your whole life, didja?"

Milchuk said yes, yes he had.

"Then maybe you can explain to my pal there what it's like to be a true fan." Carnes filled him in on the argument they had been having about the Red Sox and their alleged penury.

Penner did not think Milchuk would respond, but it may have been that Milchuk, like Penner, was using the argument to escape the turmoil of his thoughts.

"Seems to me he's gotta point." He spoke dully, as if it were a litany in which he no longer believed. "Lookit how they let Bruce Hurst get away. You gotta lefthander wins nineteen in Fenway, you don't just let him walk."

"Hurst was gone no matter what they offered," Carnes said. "Guy's a religious fanatic. He didn't go for all the shit about Boggs porkin' that cunt what's-her-name."

"That's just the excuse Gorman used." Milchuk shifted forward, warming to the subject. "Truth is, they just didn't wanta pay him. Same shit they pulled when they let Fisk jump. They claimed it was a fuck-up, they sent him his contract late. But they just didn't wanta pay the man. They couldn't say that 'cause they didn't wanta look bad, but that's how it was."

The tension in the car had dissipated to a small degree. Penner maintained vigilance, but with part of his mind he slipped beneath the moment into a warm, nurturing place. It seemed he had been liberated, that the extreme nature of what he was about had freed him of the past. His life was a transparency. It could take on any color, any condition, No longer was he required to be hopeless Penner, bankrupt Penner, pitiful, pussy-whipped Penner. He was blank, empty, a hollow shell fitted with a few basic drives. He could be anything he chose. He could escape the noose of circumstance and drive to Florida, catch a plane to Rio, grow gray-haired and eccentric on some isolated beach, companioned by canny parrots and foolish women. He could divorce not only his wife, but also his feelings for her; he could spit them out like a mouthful of tepid beer. Yet as they drew closer to the turn-off, to the place where they were to kill Milchuk, his daydream began to fray and he became less and less capable of avoiding the issue at hand. Panic grew large in him. He considered murder charges, the plight of his immortal soul, and he threw himself into the baseball argument with uncharacteristic vehemence.

"You take Burks, now," he said. "He's gotta be one of the fastest guys in the league, right?"

"That's right," said Milchuk, nodding vigorously. "You're absolutely right."

"So what is it with him? He gets on first, he looks lost. What's he got now? Seven or eight stolen bases? You figure they'd hire somebody to teach him how to steal, wouldn'tcha? But naw!" He tapped Carnes on the shoulder. "What's that alla 'bout, man? They just too damn cheap? Or is it 'cause they're fuckin' prejudiced. Maybe they're trying to make Burks look so bad they'll hafta trade him, then they can have the only all-white team in the league."

"Sox ain't prejudiced against niggers," Carnes said; from the hunched set of his neck and shoulders, Penner knew that he was fuming.

"Hear that, man?" said Penner, giving Milchuk a nudge. "They ain't prejudiced against *niggers*."

Milchuk grinned, shook his head in amusement.

"I didn't say *I* wasn't prejudiced, motherfucker!" said Carnes. "I said the Sox wasn't."

"That's garbage!" said Milchuk. "Check out the fuckin' record. If Jim Rice played his career in New York, they'd make a fuckin' statue to him. Here they just tell the guy, 'See ya later'. And even before that, the sportswriters are on his case day in, day out. I admit the guy wasn't hittin'. But Yaz, man, whenever Yaz didn't hit, the fuckin' writers acted like all they wanna do is hold the guy's prick and make him feel better."

"Damn straight," said Penner. "Fuckin' town's built on prejudice. Take what happened to Dee Brown the other day. He's the Celtics' number one pick, right? So he's sitting out front the post office in Wellesley with his fiancee. He's in his car, and he's reading his mail. He just picked it up, see. He's got an apartment not too far away. Next thing some broad in the bank across the street spots him and says, Holy shit, a Nee-gro! Why that must be the same Nee-gro robbed us a few weeks back. Makes sense, right? I mean what would a Nee-gro be doing in Wellesley he wasn't there to rob a bank? So here come the cops. Eight of 'em. They roust Brown and his girlfriend, and force 'em to lie face down on the sidewalk for twenty fucking minutes. At gunpoint, man! Twenty fucking minutes! You believe that?"

"No shit!" said Milchuk. "That's what happened, no shit?"

"It don't matter," said Carnes. "If you're a true fan, none of that crap matters."

"True fan!" said Penner disparagingly. "What the hell's that mean? The Red Sox front office screws everybody over. Fans, players. They're no different from the government, man. They do just enough to get by, just enough to confuse people into thinking it's all gonna be okay, when the fact is the storm's coming and ain't no roof on the barn. They're not gonna be able to re-sign half their fucking players, their best pitcher probably needs psychiatric help. Their manager looks like an old alcoholic and talks about his freaking vegetable garden whenever you ask him 'bout his problem at shortstop. You hafta go back to prehistory to find when's the last time they won the Series. Nineteen-fucking-eighteen! And the Celtics, man, they're just watching their players grow old. Fucking Larry Bird's starting to look like Freddy Krueger with a limp. And the Patriots...Jesus Christ! Only thing they're good at's waggling their dicks at female reporters."

They were almost at the turn-off, and a terrifying hilarity was mounting inside Penner. He heard the reediness of fear in his voice, yet he had the idea that if he kept on ranting he might accidentally work a spell that would abolish the need to kill Milchuk.

"And still you people keep going to the goddamn games," he went on, his voice shrilling. "You support this crapola. I mean nothing stops you. The fact that these assholes in three-piece suits are selling your dreams down the fucking river, it just doesn't sink in. Here they go gettin' rid of your best reliever 'cause he's black, pickin' up white guys with bad backs and dead arms, and you think it's wonderful. They lose your best pitching prospect 'cause they forget to put his name on the protected list. And whaddaya do? You boycott? You try and change anything? Fuck, no! You go on buying your dumb hats and your T-shirts, your shamrock jackets. You make stupid into a religion. Stand around chanting, Ooh, ooh, ooh whenever the team wins, like those pathetic rejects on Arsenio Hall. You don't even notice the whole thing's going down the toilet. You just sit there and babble about next year, while everything turns to shit around you. True fans, my ass! Fans appreciate the game, they can argue the finer points, y'know. They wanta win, but they don't act like lobotomy cases when they lose. They understand when they're getting jerked around. But you guys...Jesus Christ! All you guys are is a buncha fucking lemmings!"

Carnes made no sound or movement, but his anger was as palpable as heat from a open furnace. The silence grew long and prickly. The humming of the Caddy's tires seemed to register the increase of tension.

"That Lisa Olson deal," said Milchuk tentatively. "Those assholes flashin' her in the Pats locker room, that was the worst, man." He glanced at Penner, his face stamped with an expression of concern. "I ain't sayin' I don't have problems with women in the locker room, y'know, but geez!"

"Now that's terrific, that is," said Carnes. "It's really great gettin' an education on how to treat broads from the guy cornholed Lori McDonough."

A look of bewilderment washed over Milchuk's stolid face. "What're you talkin', man?"

Carnes slammed his hand against the steering wheel and shouted, "You raped her, you fuckin' Polack sleaze! You raped her, then you fucked her up the ass!"

Milchuk sat stunned for a few beats. Then he said, "Fuck I did! Hey!" He turned to Penner. "That what this is alla 'bout, man? I didn't do nothin' to Lori. I been goin' out with her six months. This is fuckin' nuts! We been talkin' 'bout gettin' married, even!"

Penner said, with unconvincing sternness, "Take it easy," and poked him with the muzzle of the gun as a reminder. He felt queasy, nauseated.

"It was Lori's old man hired you guys, wasn't it?" said Milchuk. "It hadda be. Look, I swear to fucking Christ I didn't do nothin'! It's her old man. He's against me from the start, he told me he didn't want me sniffin' around her."

"Guess you shoulda listened, huh?" said Carnes brightly.

"I didn't do nothin', man. Swear to God! All ya gotta do is to give Lori a call."

"Maybe we should," said Penner, trying to hide a certain eagerness.

"Yeah!" said Milchuk. "Call her, for Christ's sake."

"You musta done somethin'," Carnes said to Milchuk. "Maybe all you are's a pain in the ass to McDonough. But a guy like you, you musta done somethin'."

Milchuk put both hands to his face. "This is crazy," he said into his palms. "Crazy!"

"How you figure?" Penner asked of Carnes. "You don't even know the guy!"

"Oh, I know him," Carnes said. "He pals around with the Vitarellis down in Providence. He's a wise guy. You better believe the son of a bitch got blood on his hands. Whackin' him out ain't no worse than steppin' on a cockroach."

"He's with the Mob?" Penner said, incredulous. "We're supposed to hit a Mob guy?"

Without reducing his speed, Carnes swung onto a gravel road that wound away through low thickets, the leaves mostly gone to brown. The Caddy soared over bumps and ruts, landing heavily, its rear end slewing. Black branches slapped at the windows.

"Nobody said anything 'bout hitting a Mob guy!" Penner yelled.

Milchuk gripped the front seat with both hands and began talking, half-sobbing the words, offering a string of temptations and threats of Vitarelli vengeance, like a strange, primitive prayer. Carnes' only response was to increase their speed. The Caddy seemed to be trying to lift off, to go sailing up into the sky of broken silver light and black clouds. The world beyond the side windows was a chaos of tearing leaves and clawing twigs.

"So whaddaya wanna do, man?" Carnes shouted. "Wanna let him go?"

"Yes!" said Penner. "Fuckin' A, I wanna let him go!"

"Okay, say we do it, say we let him go. Know what happens next? The son of a bitch goes to the Vitarellis, he says, Chuckie, man, Chuckie, he says, that fucker McDonough tried to put a hit on me, and Chuckie says, we can't have that shit, now can we, and he sends his people up to Southie. And you know who gets it? Not McDonough. Nosir! It's you and me, buddy! We wind up on a beach somewheres with our dicks hangin' out our mouths." He swerved the Caddy around a tight bend. "We're fuckin' committed, man!"

The thickets gave way abruptly to a grassy clearing centered by the gray-shingled ruin of a one-story house, nearly roofless, with a shattered door and glassless windows; it looked out over the Atlantic toward a spit that rose at its seaward end into a pine-fringed pinnacle standing up some sixty feet above the water, the highest point of land in sight. Carnes brought the Caddy to a shuddering halt and switched off the engine. The rush of silence hurt Penner's head. Carnes turned to them, resting his elbow on the seat. A silver-plated gun dangled from his hand. He grinned at Milchuk.

"Party time," he said.

Milchuk met his eyes for a second, then hung his head. All thought of resistance seemed to have left him.

"Outside," Carnes told him, and without hesitation or objection, he opened the door and climbed out. He still clung to his briefcase, still held it against his chest. His face slack, eyes empty, he stared off over the water.

Penner slid out after him. After so many hours in the

car, standing in the open disoriented him. The world was too wide, too full of light and color; the soughing sounds of the waves and the seething wind; he could not gather it all inside him. He kept his gun trained on Milchuk.

"Drop the gun," said Carnes, coming up behind him.

Startled, Penner made to turn but stopped when the muzzle of Carnes' automatic jabbed into the side of his neck. He let the gun fall, and Carnes kicked him in the back of the legs, driving him to his knees in the tall grass. Another kick, this directly on the tailbone, sent him onto his stomach.

"Still curious 'bout why McDonough paid so much, are ya?" said Carnes. "Want me to fill ya in on the program, motherfucker?"

Penner rolled onto his back. Carnes straddled him, his feet planted on either side of Penner's thighs, automatic aimed at his chest. Milchuk, whom he could not see, was somewhere behind him.

"This here's gonna be a doubleheader, pal," said Carnes gloatingly. "Man's payin' me to whack you out, too. Betcha can't guess why."

Penner was afraid, but the fear was dim. Looking up at the muzzle of the gun, feeling the stony shoulder of earth beneath him, seeing the dark clouds wheeling like great slow wings above Carnes, he felt oddly peaceful, even sleepy. It would be all right, he thought, to close his eyes

"It's your fuckin' old lady," said Carnes. "Her and McDonough been bumpin' bellies for a year now. Whaddaya think about that, shithead?"

The news surprised Penner. And hurt him. Yet because of the numb drowsiness that had stolen over him, the hurt was slight, as if a heavy stone had been placed on his chest, making him sink deeper into the cold grass, closer to sleep. Carnes seemed disappointed in his reaction. His eyes darted elsewhere—toward Milchuk, probably—then he looked down again at Penner, a nerve jumping in his cheek.

"McDonough tells me she can't get enough of his dick,"

Carnes said. "Says her pussy's like twitchin' alla time. Says he's gonna marry the bitch."

Penner did not believe that McDonough would have confided in Carnes, but the words opened him to visions of Barbara and McDonough in bed, to the bitter comprehension that this was everything she had wanted, a man of wealth and power. He should have anticipated her choice, he should have known that McDonough would never have concocted such a simple scheme as the one he had laid out. McDonough had seen a way to kill two birds with one stone and had orchestrated it beautifully, and Penner's sadness was not only a reaction to the betrayal, but to how easily he had been taken in.

"Man, I can't tell ya how good this feels. I fuckin' cannot tell ya!" Carnes let out a lilting, girlish laugh. "I been wantin' to do you since I was fifteen fuckin' years old. Just goes to show, man. Don't never give up on your dreams." He took a shooter's grip on the automatic. "Wanna gimme some more bullshit 'bout the Sox? C'mon, man! Let's hear it! Y'ain't gonna have no chances after this."

Penner was unable to speak, and Carnes said, "What's your problem, fuckhead! This is your big moment. Talk to me!" And kicked him again.

The kick dislodged something in Penner, tipped over a little reservoir of loathing that for the moment washed away fear.

"You're fucking ridiculous!" he said. "Both you and the fuckin' Sox!"

Muscles twitched in Carnes' jaw, that weasely face jittering with hate. "I am gonna kill you a piece at a time," he said.

Something black and flat and angular—Milchuk's briefcase, Penner later realized—smacked into Carnes' gun hand and knocked it aside. The automatic discharged, the round burrowed into the earth close to Penner's cheek, spraying him with dirt. Carnes remained straddling him, and Penner was not sure if he had actually thought of kicking Carnes or if the movement of his leg had been a startled reaction to the gunshot; whatever the case, his foot drove hard into Carnes' balls. He screamed and dropped to his knees, then pitched onto his side, curling up around the pain. When Penner threw a wild punch that glanced off his shoulder, Carnes rolled away and tried to bring his gun to bear; but he was still in too much pain to function. Sucking for air, his hand trembling violently. His eyes were weepy and narrowed to slits. With his Red Sox cap and the tears, he looked like a savage, terrified little boy. Then he puked, heaving up a geyser of coffee and bad fluids.

Penner saw his own gun gleaming in the grass. Luminous with fright, he made a dive for it and came up firing. The first shot half-deafened him, ranging off somewhere into the sky, but the second hammered a red nailhead into Carnes' jacket just below the collar. The third blew bloody fragments from his lower jaw. There was no need for another.

Penner came unsteadily to his feet. His ears were ringing, his legs shaking. He gazed out over the thickets, the dry, turned leaves rippling with the same agitated motion as the chop on the water. The emptiness of the place assaulted him, and after a second, moved by a perverse need to connect with something, he staggered over to the body. The sight of the jellied eyes and ruined jaw sickened him at first and hurt his heart; but then, thinking of the man, he was furious. Carnes' Red Sox cap had fallen off, and Penner gave it a vicious kick.

Then he remembered Milchuk. He went quickly along the edge of the clearing, peering into the thickets. It was doubtful Milchuk would contact the police, but he would certainly have a talk with the Vitarellis.

After a moment he spotted him. Surfacing among the camouflage colors of the bushes. Running fast. Hurdling a fallen log. Zig-zagging around some obstacle. Moving like a halfback in the broken field. Penner might have admired his athleticism had it not been so futile—Milchuk was headed not for the highway but toward the spit of land. He must not be able to see it because of the low ground over which he was running, the bushes and a few trees obscuring his view; any moment now, however, he would realize he was trapped, that he would have to make his way along the shore. Because the spit formed the eastern enclosure of a bay, because the bay was cut back behind the clearing, the shore line lay close to where Penner was standing. He should be able to catch up to Milchuk without much difficulty.

He started toward the shore line west of the spit. He ran easily, confidently, with what seemed to him astonishing grace, turning sideways to avoid the clutches of twigs and branches. Not a misstep, not a stumble. He felt charged by this simple physical competence. It was as if the pure necessity of the moment had invoked a corresponding purity in him, eliminating all clumsiness, fear and hesitancy. But on reaching the shore he saw no sign of Milchuk, and once again he became confused.

Where the hell was he?

The sun broke through again, turning the water a steely blue, and Penner, scanning the shore line, had to shade his eyes. Milchuk had outsmarted him, he thought, he had doubled back to the clearing. But then he saw him among the pines that sprouted from the rocky point at the seaward end of the spit. Apparently, he had not seen Penner. He was just standing there, looking back toward the clearing.

Penner was baffled. What could he have in mind? Did he intend to swim for it? If so, because of Penner's position and the cut-back curve of the shoreline, he would have to swim about a mile in freezing, choppy water to the opposite side of the bay—where there was a motel and some houses—in order to insure his safety. A mile. That would take...what? At least an hour. Hypothermia would set in before then. And yet the man was obviously in excellent shape. Maybe he could make it.

But if that was the plan, why didn't he just dive in?

It took a minute's consideration before Penner understood Milchuk's tactic. From his vantage, Milchuk could see not only the clearing and the house, but also the dirt road. Perhaps even the highway itself. It would be impossible for Penner to pretend to leave; in order to persuade Milchuk to abandon his position, he would have to drive a considerable distance away, far enough to allow Milchuk to escape along the shore. If he were to try and take Milchuk on the spit, Milchuk would risk the swim; he would likely have decided how closely he would let Penner approach, and once that line was crossed, he would swim for the far side, never permitting his pursuer within pistol range. Very smooth, very economical.

The spiritual vacuum that the shooting had created in Penner was losing its integrity, filling in with vengeful thoughts concerning McDonough and Barbara, fearful thoughts of the Mafia, the police, God's justice. The idea of lying down somewhere and yielding up his fate to the operations of chance, was more than a little inviting. The inside of his head felt hot and agitated, as if his thoughts were whirling like dust, like excited atoms. But this was no time, he told himself, for his usual collapse, his usual fuck-up, and he forced himself to focus on the matter at hand.

He would not be able to kill Milchuk—he admitted to that—and eventually the Vitarellis would learn what had happened. That being the case, he could not risk returning to Southie. Well, that was okay. He had his fifty grand. And he would have Carnes' share as well. It would be a bloody business, tugging off Carne's money belt. Have to look at those eyes again, that marbled cross-section of gore and splintered bone. But he could manage it. A hundred grand would buy a lot of future in the right country. The thing to do now would be to neutralize Milchuk as much as possible so as to secure a chance at freedom. He'd ditch the Caddy in Hyannis, catch a bus into Boston. Fly out of Logan, maybe. Or buy a junker and drive south. Whatever. He could work the details out later. In the meantime, there was a flaw in Milchuk's plan...or if not a flaw, an inherent softness that he might be able to exploit. He pulled out his handkerchief, wiped off the gun with meticulous care, then wadding the handkerchief in his palm to prevent further contact with his skin, he gripped the gun by the muzzle and set out walking toward the spit. He called to Milchuk as he went, not wanting to startle him into a hasty dive. "Hey!" he shouted. "Don't be afraid, man! It's over! It's okay!"

Milchuk started down the slope of the point toward the water; he was shrugging off his overcoat.

Penner paused at the landward end of the spit; the opposite end was thirty, maybe forty yards distant.

"It's okay, man," he yelled. "Here! Look!" He waved the gun back and forth above his head. "I'm leaving this for ya! Leaving it right here!"

Milchuk stopped his descent and rested in a crouch halfway down the slope, peering at him.

Penner tossed the gun out onto the spit, surreptitiously pocketed his handkerchief. "I'm outta here, okay? No more shooting! No more bullshit!"

Being unarmed made him feel exposed, but he knew that Milchuk would wait until he had retreated more than a pistol shot away before going after the gun. More likely he'd wait until he watched the Caddy pull down the highway. There would be plenty of time for Penner to make it back to the clearing and collect Carnes' money and his gun.

"You hear me?" Penner called.

A beam of sunlight fingered Milchuk among the stones, accentuating his isolation and the furtiveness of his pose. The sight caught at Penner. He could not help but sympathize with the man.

"If you hear me," he called, "gimme a sign! Okay?"

Milchuk remained motionless for a bit, then—reluctantly, it seemed—lifted his right arm as if in salute; after a second he let it fall back heavily. The sun withdrew behind the clouds, and he was reduced to a dark primitive form hunkered among the rocks. Behind him, toiling masses of black and silver muscled toward the top of the sky, and the sea, dark as iron, moved in a vast, uneasy swell, as if the entire world had been nudged sideways.

"Okay, I'm outta here!" Penner half-turned away, and then, moved by a fleeting morality, a vestigial remnant of innocence, he shouted, "Hey! Good luck!" It amazed him, the sincerity he had felt while saying it.

Penner was more than satisfied with his performance during the phone call to the police. He had exhibited, he thought, just the right mix of paranoia and breathless excitement.

"The little guy knew the shooter," he'd said. "I heard him say the bastard's name, anyway. Millbuck, Mil...something. I don't know. He might still be around there, man, you hurry."

After hanging up, he decided to get some coffee before hitting the highway, but as he stepped around the corner from the pay phone into the dining area of the roadside MacDonald's, through the window he saw a green Buick pull up behind the Caddy, blocking it in. Two men climbed out of the Buick. Beefy, florid men, one—the taller—balding, with a fringe of dark hair curling low on his neck, and the other with straight red hair falling over his collar. Irish-looking men. Cops, was Penner's first thought; they must have traced the call. But then he realized that their hair was too long, their suits too expensive. They peered in the windows of the Caddy, at the hood, exchanged a few words; then the red-haired man slid back into the Buick and drove it into a parking space. The other made for the front door.

A weight shifted loosely in Penner's bowels. Christ, he should have figured! McDonough could not allow a loose cannon like Carnes to jeopardize his position. Carnes had likely been instructed to drive somewhere after the job, to follow some specific course; these men had been set to meet him, and—no doubt—to dispatch him and reclaim the money. The advance payment made perfect sense now.

Wrong again, Carnes.

We're talking a tripleheader here.

Beautiful, thought Penner. This was McDonough functioning at the peak of his political acumen. Minimal involvement of his people. Minimal risk to himself. A neat system of checks and balances. Snick, snick, snick. Three problems solved, all's right with the world, and the great man could look forward to a lubricious future with the former Mrs. Penner. After an appropriate period of mourning, of course. What a player he was! What a master of the fucking game!

Penner retreated around the corner. The primary colors of the walls were making his skin hot, and the merry babble of the diners generated a fuming commotion inside his head. Hostages, he thought. Grab somebody off line, drag them into the parking lot. The idea had an outlaw charm that appealed to the absurdist witness who seemed to be sharing the experience with him. Mad Dog Penner. But instead, he ducked into the bathroom. The windows were high and narrow. A skinny dwarf might have managed an escape. He flattened against the wall behind the door, holding Carnes' gun muzzle-up beside his cheek. The white tiles were vibrating. The stainless steel fixtures glowed like treasure. Every living gleam was a splinter in his eye. His thoughts were singing. Oh, Jesus Jesus Jesus please! What if some cute little tyke comes in to take his first solo piss, and you splatter the wee fuck's brains all over the hand drier? God, let me live, I'll say a billion Hail Marys, I swear it, right here in this holy nowhere of a bathroom I'm opening myself up to You, this is one of Your chosen speaking, an Irishman, a former acolyte, as sorry a lamb as ever strayed, and I'm begging, no, I'm fucking demanding a religious experience!

The big, balding man pushed into the bathroom, his entrance accompanied by a venting of happy chatter from the restaurant, and said "Shit" under his breath. He bent with hands-on-knees to peek beneath the doors of the stalls, exposing the back of his head. Joy surged in Penner's heart on seeing that tonsured bull's-eye, and as the man straightened, he stepped forward and smashed the gun butt against his scalp. The blow made a plush, heavy sound that alarmed him. But he struck again as the man toppled, rills of blood webbing the patch of mottled skin, and then dropped to his knees beside the man and struck a third time. He remained kneeling there with gun held high, like a child who has hit a spider with a shoe and is watching to see if its legs wiggle. More blood was pooling inside the man's ear. Penner's mind went skittering, unable to seize upon a thought. The white tiles seemed to be exuding a thick silence.

The red-haired man, he said to himself at last; he would exercise extreme caution when his friend failed to reappear. Nothing to be gained by waiting for him. He, Penner, would have to balls it out. Take a stroll off into Ronald McDonaldland and see what we can see. Tra la. He laughed, and the hollowness of the sound sobered him a touch, heightened his alertness. He caught the handle of a stall door and pulled himself up.

"Stay right there," he told the balding man, and gave him a wink. "One false move, and I'll hafta plug ya."

He squared his shoulders, took a deep breath. Maybe they were still looking for Carnes, maybe the red-haired man wouldn't recognize him. Who could say on a day like today? He stuffed the gun into the pocket of his windbreaker. He felt giddy, but the giddiness acted as a restorative, a nervy drug that encouraged him.

"Yoicks," he said. "Tally ho!"

It was a fabulous day in Ronald McDonaldland. The sun had come out, the restaurant was thronged with golden light and pleasant smells, young secretaries and construction workers were stuffing Egg McMuffins into their mouths, and the red-haired man was just turning from the line of waiting customers when Penner stepped up and let him feel the gun in his side.

"Why don't we take a walk outside?" Penner said. "I mean that's what *I'd* like to do. But I don't really care what happens, so you choose, okay?"

The man scarcely hesitated before obeying. The act of

a professional, thought Penner, submitting by course to the rule of might. Beautiful.

They pushed through the glass doors out into the sun. The freshness and brightness of the air infected Penner, making him incredibly light and easy on his feet. Life was everywhere in him, plumping out all his hollows. The poor dead, he said to himself, not to have this, not to know. He felt like weeping, like singing.

"What's the story here?" he asked, screwing the muzzle of Carnes' gun deeper into the man's side. "How'd you find me?"

"You kiddin'?" said the man. "You drivin' a Cadillac with vanity plates and a pair of red socks painted on the hood, you think you're hard to find?"

His disdainful attitude unnerved Penner.

"Where's Carnes?" the man asked.

"Ah, well, now," Penner said blithely. "That's one for the philosophers, that is."

He forced the man to deposit his gun in the dumpster at the side of the building. The man's doughy face registered an almost comical degree of worry, and Penner considered telling him everything was going to work out, but realized that the man would not believe him. Instead, he asked for the keys to the Buick.

"Beautiful," he said, accepting the keys, and pushed the man forward, moving through the asphalt dimension of the parking lot, the humming of traffic, like the dark general noise of life itself.

He had the man sit on the floor of the front seat with his back to the engine, his head wedged under the dash, legs stuck between the seat and the side panel. A tight fit, but the man managed it. It pleased Penner to have devised this clever prison.

"Comfy?" he asked.

The man gave no reply.

Driving also pleased Penner. In the golden light the cars shone with the luster of gemstones under water, and he cut in and out of traffic with the flash of a Petty, a

Yarborough. Lapping the field in the Penner 500.

What to do, what to do, he thought.

South on I-93 to New York, Washington, Miami and points beyond?

Brazil?

Just the place, so they said, for a man with a gun on the run.

He let the rhyme sing inside his head for a minute or so, liking the erratic spin it lent to all his thoughts. He switched on the radio. He heard the amplified crack of a bat and brash music. Then a man's voice blatted from the speaker, saying that his guest was Mike Greenwell of the Boston Red Sox. Penner had to laugh.

"What the fuck's goin' on?" asked the red-haired man; he crooked his head to the side so he could get a look at Penner.

"You gotta name?" Penner asked.

"Yeah...Tom," said the man with bad grace.

"You a Sox fan, Tom?"

The man said, "What?"

"I said you a Sox fan? It's not a trick question."

Silence.

"Know what I think about the Sox, Tom? They're God's baseball joke. A metaphor for man's futility. The Sisyphus of the American League East."

The man's face showed no sign of comprehension. His eyes were flat and regarding. A serpent, Penner thought. There is a serpent in my garden.

"Where's McDonough?" Penner asked him.

More silence.

"Now you don't *have* to answer." Penner jabbed the muzzle of the gun into the man's belly. "But I just bet he's waiting for a call from you."

"Home," said the man. "He's at home."

"Anyone with him? A woman, maybe?"

"How the fuck should I know?"

"Right," said Penner, pulling back the gun. "How, indeed?"

But Penner knew his Barbara. She would be with McDonough. She was part of this. And she would be able to live with it, to make that kind of moral trade-off. He experienced a hiccup of emotion and pictured pale limbs asprawl, a gory tunnel burrowed into a shock of white hair. Could he really waste them? he wondered. How would it feel? Amazingly enough, it had felt pretty damn good so far. Since blood from the ears was not considered a healthy sign, he figured his score for the day was two. Four would not be a problem.

But, after all, it would be nice to survive this. As Barbara herself was wont to say, the best revenge was living well.

He had not, he realized, been considering the prospect of survival until this moment. Not really. Not with the calculation you needed to weigh the possibilities, nor with the calmness necessary to believe in them.

On the radio Mike Greenwell was saying there was no reason to panic, they just had to take 'em one at a time.

Sound philosophy, Mike. Words to live by.

A pick-up truck roared past, somebody screamed a curse at Penner. He noticed that he had let the speed of the car drop to thirty.

Brazil.

Take the money and run. What could be the problem with that?

He caught movement out of the corner of his eye. Ol' Tom shifting about ever so slightly, preparing to try and kick the gun. Penner couldn't much blame him for trying—unless he were a cockeyed optimist, he could not like his chances very much. He had proved a surly bastard, had Tom, and Penner elected not to extend him a warning.

The problem, he decided, making an effort to concentrate, the problem was in himself. In the Penner he always ended up being, no matter how promising the circumstance. Sad, sorrowful, Penner. Christ the Penner inevitably borne toward some unimportant Passion.

But that, he thought, was the old Penner, the bumbling,

good-hearted villain, the con man with a conscience.

Who was he now? he wondered. Was this Penner any better off?

Hot, he thought. Excessive heating of the face and palms seemed the primary characteristic of this particular Penner. A few aches and pains, a desire for an end to all this. Otherwise, very little to report. Pared down to almost nothing.

"You can't do better than your best," Mike Greenwell was saying. "You give a hunnerd and fifty percent, you got no reason to hang your head."

Amen to that, Mike.

The red-haired man had worked a leg up onto the seat, and Penner thought a confrontation might be just the way to decide such a momentous issue as one's future or the lack thereof. Let him make his play. If Penner won, he would do...something. He'd figure out exactly what later.

Despite the indecisiveness of this resolution, Penner felt there was a fine weight to it, an Irish logic that defied interpretation. To make things interesting, he boosted their speed to 50. Then to 60. He kept pressing his foot harder on the gas, watching the needle climb, feeling that the speed was the result of him being pulled toward something. There was a curve coming up about a mile ahead, and he wondered how it would be just to keep going straight when he reached it. To go arcing up into stormlight over the water, into the golden glare and big-muscled clouds. And then down.

Do I hear any objections? he asked himself.

Fucking A, I object, he answered. Fuck all that remorseful Catholic bullshit! This is your goddamn life, Penner. This is the Hundred Thousand Dollar Challenge! Are you man enough to accept it?

"You play a hunnerd and sixty-two games," Mike Greenwell said, "you gotta expect a few bad days. But we'll be there in the end."

Dead on, Mike me boyo!

Penner could tell that the red-haired man was waiting

for him to look away, to do something that would give him an advantage; but that was no longer a problem. The game was in hand, and all the signs were auspicious. Light was flowing around the car, fountaining up behind in an incandescent wake, and the green world was blurring with their momentum, and the corners of Penner's mind were sharp and bright as never before. Life hot as a magnesium flare, as Brazil, as freedom and the future, all the love in him sizzling high. He boosted their speed to 65 as they approached the curve, enjoying the feeling of being on the edge.

"Hey!" said the red-haired man; he had curled his fingers about the door handle, his eyes were round with fright. "Hey, you're going too fast!"

The old Penner might have lied, made a gentle promise, offered hope or perhaps spoken persuasively of the afterlife. But this was not the old Penner.

Far from it.

"Not me," said the Wild Blue-Eyed Penner, lifting his gun. As the Caddy swung into the sweet gravity of the curve, he trained the gun at his enemy's heart, seeing only an interruption of the light, a dark keyhole set in a golden door. The thunderous report and the kick made it seem that the man's life had traveled up his arm, charging him with a fierce new spirit. He took in the sight without flinching. Blood as red as paper roses. The body with its slack, twisted limbs looked larger than before, more solid, as if death were in essence a kind of important stillness. He stared at it until he was completely at ease. A smile sliced his face, the sort of intent expression that comes from peering into strong sunlight or hard weather. He thought about the disposal problem, a passport, opportunities for tropical investment. He spun the tuning dial, found an easy listening station. Paul Simon was going to Graceland, and he was going with him.

"Not me," said Penner the Implacable, the Conscienceless, the Almost Nothing Man. "I'm just hitting my stride."

a little night music

"Dead men can't play jazz.

"That's the truth I learned last night at the world premiere performance of the quartet known as Afterlife at Manhattan's Village Vanguard.

"Whether or not they can play, period, that's another matter, but it wasn't jazz I heard at the Vanguard, it was something bluer and colder, something with notes made from centuries-old Arctic ice and stones that never saw the light of day, something uncoiling after a long black sleep and tasting dirt in its mouth, something that wasn't the product of creative impulse but of need.

"But the bottom line is, it was worth hearing.

"As to the morality involved, well, I'll leave that up to you, because that's the real bottom line, isn't it, music lovers? Do you like it enough and will you pay enough to keep the question of morality a hot topic on the Donahue show and out of the courts? Those of you who listened to the simulcast over WBAI have probably already formulated an opinion. The rest of you will have to wait for the CD.

"I won't waste your time by talking about the technology. If you don't understand it by now, after all the television specials and the (ohmygodpleasenotanother) in-depth discussions between your local blowdried news creep and their pet science fiction hack, you must not want to understand it. Nor am I going to wax profound and speculate on just how much of a man is left after reanimation. The only ones who know that aren't able to tell us, because it seems the speech center just doesn't thrive on narcosis. Nor does any fraction of sensibility that cares to communicate itself. In fact, very little seems to thrive on narcosis aside from the desire...no, like I said, the *need* to play music.

"And for reasons that God or someone only knows, the *ability* to play music where none existed before.

"That may be hard to swallow, I realize, but I'm here to tell you, no matter how weird it sounds, it appears to be true.

"For the first time in memory, there was a curtain across the Vanguard's stage. I suppose there's some awkwardness involved in bringing the musicians out. Before the curtain was opened, William Dexter, the genius behind this whole deal, a little bald man with a hearing aid in each ear and the affable, simple face of someone who kids call by his first name, came out and said a few words about the need for drastic solutions to the problems of war and pollution, for a redefinition of our goals and values. Things could not go on as they had been. The words seemed somewhat out of context, though they're always nice to hear. Finally he introduced the quartet. As introductions go, this was a telegram.

"'The music you're about to hear,' William Dexter said

flatly, without the least hint of hype or hyperventilation, 'is going to change your lives.'

"And they were.

"Right on the same stage where Coltrane turned a love supreme into song, where Miles singed us with the hateful beauty of needles and knives and Watts on fire, where Mingus went crazy in 7/4 time, where Ornette made Kansas City R&B into the art of noise, and a thousand lesser geniuses dreamed and almost died and were changed before our eyes from men into moments so powerful that guys like me can make a living writing about them for people like you who just want to hear that what they felt when they were listening was real.

"Two white men, one black, one Hispanic, the racial quota of an all-American TV show, marooned on a radiant island painted by a blue-white spot. All wearing sunglasses.

"Raybans, I think.

"Wonder if they'll get a commercial.

"The piano player was young and skinny, just a kid, with the long brown hair of a rock star and sunglasses that held gleams as shiny and cold as the black surface of his Baldwin. The Hispanic guy on bass couldn't have been more than eighteen, and the horn player, the black man, he was about twenty-five, the oldest. The drummer, a shadow with a crewcut and a pale brow, I couldn't see him clearly but I could tell he was young, too.

"Too young, you'd think, to have much to say.

"But then maybe time goes by more slowly and wisdom accretes with every measure...in the afterlife.

"No apparent signal passed between them, yet as one they began to play."

Goodrick reached for his tape recorder, thinking he should listen to the set again before getting into the music, but then he realized that another listen was unnecessary—he could still hear every blessed note. The ocean of dark chords on the piano opening over a snaky, slithering hiss of cymbals and a cluttered rumble plucked from the double bass, and then that sinuous alto line, like snake charmer music rising out of a storm of thunderheads and scuttling claws, all fusing into a signature as plaintive and familiar and elusive as a muezzin's call. Christ, it stuck with you like a jingle for Burger King...though nothing about it was simple. It seemed to have the freedom of jazz, yet at the same time it had the feel of heavy, ritual music.

Weird shit.

And it sure as hell stuck with you.

He got up from the desk, grabbed his drink and walked over to the window. The nearby buildings ordered the black sky, ranks of tombstones inscribed with a writing of rectangular stars, geometric constellations, and linear rivers of light below, flowing along consecutive chasms through the high country of Manhattan. Usually the view soothed him and turned his thoughts to pleasurable agendas, as if height itself were a form of assurance, an emblematic potency that freed you from anxiety. But tonight he remained unaffected. The sky and the city seemed to have lost their scope and grandeur, to have become merely an adjunct to his living room.

He cast about the apartment, looking for the clock. Couldn't locate it for a second among a chaos of sticks of gleaming chrome, shining black floors, framed prints, and the black plush coffins of the sofas. He'd never put it together before, but the place looked like a cross between a Nautilus gym and a goddamn mortuary.

Two-thirty AM...Damn!

Where the hell was she?

She usually gave him time alone after a show to write his column. Went and had a drink with friends.

Three hours, though.

Maybe she'd found a special friend. Maybe that was the reason she had missed the show tonight. If that was the case, she'd been with the bastard for...what? Almost seven hours now. Screwing her brains out in some mid-town hotel.

Bitch! He'd settle her hash when she got home.

Whoa, big fella, he said to himself. Get real. Rachel

would be much cooler than that...make that, *had been* much cooler. Her affairs were state of the art, so quietly and elegantly handled that he had been able to perfect denial. This wasn't her style. And even if she were to throw it in his face, he wouldn't do a thing to her. Oh, he'd want to, he'd want to bash her goddamned head in. But he would just sit there and smile and buy her bullshit explanation.

Love, he guessed you'd call it, the kind of love that will accept any insult, any injury...though it might be more accurate to call it pussywhipped. There were times he didn't think he could take it anymore. Times like now when his head felt full of lightning, on the verge of exploding and setting everything around him on fire. But he always managed to contain his anger and swallow his pride, to grin and bear it, to settle for the specious currency of her lovemaking, the price she paid to live high and do what she wanted.

Jesus, he felt strange. Too many pops at the Vanguard, that was likely the problem. But maybe he was coming down with something.

He laughed.

Like maybe middle age? Like the married-to-a-chick-fifteen-years-younger-paranoid flu?

Still, he had felt better in his time. No real symptoms, just out of sorts, sluggish, dulled, some trouble concentrating.

Finish the column, he said to himself, just finish the damn thing, take two aspirin and fall out. Deal with Rachel in the morning.

Right.

Deal with her.

Bring her breakfast in bed, ask how she was feeling, and what was she doing later?

God, he loved her!

Loves her not. Loves. Loves her not.

He tore off a last mental petal and tossed the stem away. Then he returned to the desk and typed a few lines about the music onto the computer and sat considering the screen. After a moment he began to type again.

"Plenty of blind men have played the Vanguard, and plenty of men have played there who've had other reasons to hide their eyes, working behind some miracle of modern chemistry that made them sensitive to light. I've never wanted to see their eyes—the fact that they were hidden told me all I need to know about them. But tonight I wanted to see, I wanted to know what the quartet was seeing, what lay behind those sunglasses starred from the white spot. Shadows, it's said. But what sort of shadows? Shades of gray, like dogs see? Are we shadows to them, or do they see shadows where we see none? I thought if I could look into their eyes, I'd understand what caused the alto to sound like a reedy alarm being given against a crawl of background radiation, why one moment it conjured images of static red flashes amid black mountains moving, and the next brought to mind a livid blue streak pulsing in a serene darkness, a mineral moon in a granite sky,

"Despite the compelling quality of the music, I couldn't set aside my curiosity and simply listen. What was I listening to, after all? A clever parlor trick? Sleight of hand on a metaphysical level? Were these guys really playing Death's Top Forty, or had Mr. William Dexter managed to chump the whole world and program four stiffs to make certain muscular reactions to subliminal stimuli?"

The funny thing was, Goodrick thought, now he couldn't stop listening to the damn music. In fact, certain phrases were becoming so insistent, circling round and round inside his head, he was having difficulty thinking rationally. He switched the radio on, wanting to hear something else, to get a perspective on the column.

No chance.

Afterlife was playing on the radio, too.

He was stunned, imagining some bizarre *Twilight Zone* circumstance, but then realized that the radio was tuned to WBAI. They must be replaying the simulcast. Pretty unusual for them to devote so much air to one story. Still, it wasn't everyday the dead came back to life and played song stylings for your listening pleasure.

He recognized the passage.

They must have just have started the replay. Shit, the boys hadn't even gotten warmed up yet.

Heh, heh.

He followed the serpentine track of the alto cutting across the rumble and clutter of the chords and fills behind it, a bright ribbon of sound etched through thunder and power and darkness.

A moment later he looked at the clock and was startled to discover that the moment had lasted twenty minutes.

Well, so he was a little spaced, so what? He was entitled. He'd had a hard wife...life. Wife. The knifing word he'd wed, the dull flesh, the syrupy blood, the pouty breasts, the painted face he'd thought was pretty. The dead music woman, the woman whose voice caused cancer, whose kisses left damp mildewed stains, whose. . .

His heart beat flabbily, his hands were cramped, his fingertips were numb, and his thoughts were a whining, glowing crack opening in a smoky sky like slow lightning. Feeling a dark red emotion too contemplative to be anger, he typed a single paragraph and then stopped to read what he had written.

"The thing about this music is, it just feels right. It's not art, it's not beauty, it's a meter reading on the state of the soul, of the world. It's the bottom line of all time. A registering of creepy fundamentals, the rendering into music of the crummiest truth, the statement of some meager final tolerance, a universal alpha wave, God's EKG, the least possible music, the absolute minimum of sound, all that's left to say, to be, for them, for us...maybe that's why it feels so damn right. It creates an option to suicide, a place where there is no great trouble, only a trickle of blood through stony flesh and the crackle of a base electric message across the brain."

Well, he thought, now there's a waste of a paragraph. Put that into the column, and he'd be looking for work with a weekly shopping guide. Hey, who knows, it might not be so bad, writing about fabric bargains and turkey raffles and swap meets. Might put him back in touch with his roots.

He essayed a laugh and produced a gulping noise.

Damn, he felt lousy

Not lousy, really, just...just sort of nothing. Like there was nothing in his head except the music. Music and black dead air. Dead life.

Dead love.

He typed a few more lines.

"Maybe Dexter was right, maybe this music *will* change your life. It sure as hell seems to have changed mine. I feel like shit, my lady's out with some dirtball lowlife and all I can muster by way of a reaction is mild pique. That's a goddamn change, sure enough. I mean, maybe the effect of Afterlife's music is to reduce the emotional volatility of our kind, to diminish us to the level of the stiffs who play it. That might explain Dexter's peace-and-love rap, put it into a cautionary context. People who feel like I do wouldn't have the energy for war, for polluting, for much of anything. They'd probably sit around most of the time, trying to think something, hoping for food to walk in the door..."

Jesus, what if the music actually did buzz you like that? Tripped some chemical switch and slowly shut you down, brain cell by brain cell, until you were about three degrees below normal and as lively as a hibernating bear. What if that was true, and right this second it was being broadcast all over hell on WBAI?

This is crazy, man, he told himself, this is truly whacko.

But what if Dexter's hearing aids had been ear plugs, what if the son of a bitch hadn't listened to the music himself? Maybe that speech of his had been more than cautionary. What if he knew how the music would effect the audience, what if he was after turning half of everybody into zombies all in the name of a better world?

And what would be so wrong with that?

Not a thing.

Cleaner air, less war, more food to go around...just stack the dim bulbs in warehouses and let them vegetate, while everyone else cleaned up the mess.

Not a thing wrong with it...as long as you weren't in the half that had listened to the music.

The light was beginning to hurt his eyes. He switched off the lamp and sat in the darkness, staring at the glowing screen. He glanced out the window. Since last he'd looked, it appeared that about three-quarters of the lights in the adjoining buildings had been darkened, making it appear that the remaining lights were some sort of weird code, spelling out a message of golden squares against a black page. He had a crawly feeling along his spine, imagining thousands of other Manhattan nighthawks growing slow and cold and sensitive to light, sitting in their dark rooms, while a whining alto serpent stung them in the brain.

The idea was ludicrous—Dexter had just been shooting off his mouth, firing off more white liberal bullshit. He was no mad scientist, no deviant little monster with a master plan.

Still, Goodrick didn't feel much like laughing.

Maybe, he thought, he should call the police...call someone.

But then he'd have to get up, dial the phone, talk, and it was so much more pleasant just to sit here and listen to the background static of the universe, to the sad song of a next-to-nothing life.

He remembered how peaceful Afterlife had been, the piano man's pale hands flowing over the keys, like white animals gliding, making a rippling track, and the horn man's eyes rolled up, showing all white under the sunglasses, turned inward toward some pacific vision, and the bass man, fingers blurring on the strings, but his head fallen back, gaping, his eyes on the ceiling, as if keeping track of the stars.

This was really happening, he thought, he believed it was happening, he knew it, and yet he couldn't rouse himself to panic. His hands flexed on the arms of the chair, and he swallowed, and he listened. More lights were switched off in the adjoining towers. This was really fucking happening...and he wasn't afraid. As a matter of fact, he was beginning to enjoy the feeling. Like a little vacation. Just turn down the volume and response, sit back and let the ol' brain start to mellow like aging cheese.

Wonder what Rachel would have to say?

Why, she'd be delighted! She hadn't heard the music, after all, and she'd be happy as a goddamn clam to be one of the quick, to have him sit there and fester while she brought over strangers and let them pork her on the living room carpet. I mean, he wouldn't have any objection, right? Maybe dead guys liked to watch. Maybe...His hands started itching, smudged with city dirt. He decided that he had to wash them. Couldn't just sit there and shit himself.

With a mighty effort, feeling like he weighed five hundred pounds, he heaved up to his feet and shuffled toward the bathroom. It took him what seemed a couple of minutes to reach it, to fumble for the wall switch and flick it on. The light almost blinded him, and he reeled back against the wall, shading his eyes. Glints and gleams shattering off porcelain, chrome fixtures, and tiles, a shrapnel of light blowing toward his retinas. "Aw, Jesus," he said. "Jesus!" Then he caught sight of himself in the mirror. Pasty skin, liverish, too-red lips, bruised-looking circles around his eyes. Mr. Zombie, he said to himself, is attired in a charcoal gray suit with Mediterranean lapels by Calvin Swine, his silk rep tie is by Necktie Party, his coral shirt is made of silk and pigeon blood, his shoes are actually layers of filthy dead skin wrinkled into an alligator pattern, and his accessories are by Mr. Mort U. Ary.

At last he managed to look away.

He turned on the faucet. Music ran out along with the bright water, and when he stuck his hands under the flow, he couldn't feel the cold water, just the gloomy notation spidering across his skin.

He jerked his hands back and stared at them, watch them dripping glittering bits of alto and drum, bass and piano. After a moment he switched off the light and stood in the cool, blessed dark, listening to the alto playing in the distance, luring his thoughts down and down into a golden crooked tunnel leading nowhere.

One thing he had to admit, having your vitality turned down to the bottom notch gave you perspective on the whole vital world. Take Rachel, now. She'd come in any minute, all bright and smiling, switching her ass, she'd toss her purse and coat somewhere, give him a perky kiss, ask how the column was going...and all the while her sexual engine would be cooling, ticking away the last degrees of heat like how a car engine ticks in the silence of a garage, some vile juice leaking from her. He could see it clearly, the entire spectrum of her deceit, see it without feeling either helpless rage or frustration, but rather registering it as an untenable state of affairs. Something would have to be done. That was obvious. It was surprising he'd never come to that conclusion before...or maybe not so surprising. He'd been too agitated, too emotional. Now...now change was possible. He would have to talk to Rachel, to work things out differently.

Actually, he thought, a talk wouldn't be necessary

Just a little listening experience, and she'd get with the program.

He hated to leave the soothing darkness of the bathroom, but he felt he should finish the column...just to tie up loose ends. He went back into the living room and sat in front of the computer. WBAI had finished replaying the simulcast. He must have been in the john a long time. He switched off the radio so he could hear the music in his head.

"I'm sitting here listening to a little night music, a reedy little whisper of melody leaking out a crack in death's door, and you know, even though I can't hear or think of much of anything except that shivery sliver of sound, it's become more a virtue than a hindrance, it's beginning to order the world in an entirely new way. I don't have to explain it to those of you who are hearing it with me, but for the rest of you, let me shed some light on the experience. One sees...clearly, I suppose, is the word, yet that doesn't cover it. One is freed from the tangles of inhibition, volatile emotion, and thus can perceive how easy it is to change one's life, and finally, one understands that with a very few changes one can achieve a state of calm perfection. A snip here, a tuck taken there, another snip-snip, and suddenly it becomes apparent that there is nothing left to do, absolutely nothing, and one has achieved utter harmony with one's environment."

The screen was glowing too brightly to look at. Goodrick dimmed it. Even the darkness, he realized, had its own peculiar radiance. B-zarre. He drew a deep breath...or rather tried to, but his chest didn't move. Cool, he thought, very cool. No moving parts. Just solid calm, white, white calm in a black, black, shell, and a little bit of fixing up remaining to do. He was almost there.

Wherever *there* was.

A cool alto trickle of pleasure through the rumble of nights.

"I cannot recommend the experience too highly. After all, there's almost no overhead, no troublesome desires, no ugly moods, no loathesome habits..."

A click—the front door opening, a sound that seemed to increase the brightness in the room. Footsteps, and then Rachel's voice

"Wade?"

He could feel her. Hot, sticky, soft. He could feel the suety weights of her breasts, the torsion of her hips, the flexing of live sinews, like music of a kind, a lewd concerto of vitality and deceit.

"There you are!" she said brightly, a streak of hot sound, and came up behind him. She leaned down, hands on his shoulders, and kissed his cheek, a serpent of brown hair coiling across his neck and onto his chest. He could hardly smell her perfume, just a hint of it. Perfect. She drenched herself in the stuff, and usually he had big trouble breathing around her, choking on the flowery reek.

"How's the column going?" she asked, moving away.

He cut his eyes toward her. That teardrop ass sheathed in silk, that mind like a sewer running with black bile, that heart like a pound of red raw poisoned hamburger. Those cute little puppies bounding along in front.

He remembered how she'd used to wear her hair up, wear aprons, just like ol' Wilma Flintstone, how he'd come home and pretend to be an adulterous Barney Rubble.

How they'd laughed.

Yabba dabba doo.

And now the fevered temperature of her soiled flesh brightened everything. Even the air was shining. The shadows were black glares.

"Fine," he said. "Almost finished."

"...only infinite slow minutes, slow thoughts like curls of smoke, only time, only a flicker of presence, only perfect music that does not exist like smoke..."

"So how was the Vanguard?"

He chuckled. "Didn't you catch it on the radio?"

A pause. "No, I was busy."

Busy, uh-huh.

Hips thrusting up from a rumpled sheet, sleek with sweat, mouth full of tongue, breasts rolling fatly, big ass flattening.

"It was food for me," he said.

A nervous giggle.

"Very good," he said. "The best ever."

He examined his feelings. All in order, all under control...what there was of them. A few splinters of despair, a fragment of anger, some shards of love. Not enough to matter, not enough to impair judgment.

"Are you okay? You sound funny."

"I'm fine," he said, feeling a creepy, secretive tingle of delight. "Want to hear the Vanguard set? I taped it."

"Sure...but aren't you sleepy? I can hear it tomorrow."

"I'm fine."

He switched on the recorder. The computer screen was blazing like a white sun.

"...the crackling of a black storm, the red thread of a fire on a distant ridge, the whole world irradiated by a mystic vibration, the quickened inches of the flesh becoming cool and easy, the White Nile of the calmed mind flowing everywhere..."

"Like it?" he asked.

She had walked over to the window and was standing facing it, gazing out at the city.

"It's...curious," she said. "I don't know if I like it, but it's effective."

Was that a hint of entranced dullness in her voice? Or was it merely distraction?

Open those ears wide, baby, and let that ol' black magic take over.

"...just listen, just let it flow in, let it fill the empty spaces in your brain with muttering, cluttering bassy blunders and a crooked wire of brassy red snake fluid, let it cozy around and coil up inside you skull, because it's all you know, America, and all you fucking need to know, Keatsian beauty and truth wrapped up in a freaky little melody..."

The column just couldn't hold his interest. Who the hell was going to read it, anyway? His place was with Rachel, helping her through the rough spots of the transition, the confusion, the unsettled feelings. With difficulty, he got to his feet and walked over to Rachel. Put his hands on her hips. She tensed, then relaxed against him. Then she tensed again. He looked out over the top of her head at Manhattan. Only a few lights showing. The message growing simpler and simpler. Dot, dot, dot. Stop. Dot, dot. Stop.

Stop.

"Can we talk, Wade?"

"Listen to the music, baby."

"No...really. We have to talk!"

She tried to pull away from him, but he held her, his fingers hooked on her hipbones.

"It'll keep 'til morning," he said.

"I don't think so." She turned to face him, fixed him

with her intricate green eyes. "I've been putting this off too long already." Her mouth opened, as if she were going to speak, but then she looked away. "I'm so sorry," she said after a considerable pause.

He knew what was coming, and he didn't want to hear it. Couldn't she just wait? In a few minutes she'd begin to understand, to know what he knew. Christ, couldn't she wait?

"Listen," he said. "Okay? Listen to the music and then we'll talk."

"God, Wade! What is it with you and this dumb music?"

She started to flounce off, but he caught her by the arm.

"If you give it a chance, you'll see what I mean," he said. "But it takes a while. You have to give it time."

"What are you talking about?"

"The music...it's really something. It does something."

"Oh, God, Wade! This is important!"

She fought against his grip.

"I know," he said, "I know it is. But just do this first. Do it for me."

"All right, all right! If it'll make you happy." She heaved a sigh, made a visible effort at focusing on the music, her head tipped to the side...but only for a couple of seconds.

"I can't listen," she said. "There's too much on my mind."

"You're not trying."

"Oh, Wade," she said, her chin quivering, a catch in her voice. "I've been trying, I really have. You don't know. Please! Let's just sit down and..." She let out another sigh. "Please. I need to talk with you."

He had to calm her, to let his calm generate and flow inside her. He put a hand on the back of her neck, forced her head down onto his shoulder. She struggled, but he kept up a firm pressure.

"Let me go, damn it!" she said, her voice muffled. "Let me go!" Then, after a moment: "You're smothering me."

He let her lift her head.

"What's wrong with you, Wade?"

There was confusion and fright in her face, and he wanted to soothe her, to take away all her anxieties.

"Nothing's wrong," he said with the sedated piety of a priest. "I just want you to listen. Tomorrow morning we..."

"I don't want to listen. Can't you understand that? I don't. Want. To listen. Now let me go."

"I'm doing this for you, baby."

"For me? Are you nuts? Let me go!"

"I can't, baby. I just can't."

She tried to twist free again, but he refused to release her.

"All right, all right! I was trying to avoid a scene, but if that's how you want it!" She tossed back her hair, glared at him defiantly. "I'm leaving..."

He couldn't let her say it and spoil the evening, he couldn't let her disrupt the healing process. Without anger, without bitterness, but rather with the precision and control of someone trimming a hedge, he backhanded her, nailed her flush on the jaw with all his strength, snapping her head about. She went hard against the thick window glass, the back of her skull impacting with a sharp crack, and then she slumped to the floor, her head twisted at an improbable angle.

Snip, snip.

He stood waiting for grief and fear to flood in, but he felt only a wave of serenity as palpable as a steam of cool water, as a cool golden passage on a distant horn.

Snip.

The shape of his life was perfected.

Rachel's too.

Lying there, pale lips parted, face rapt and slack, drained of lust and emotions, she was beautiful. A trickle of blood reeled from her hairline, and Goodrick realized that the pattern it made echoed the alto line exactly, that the music was leaking from her, signalling the minimal continuance of her life. She wasn't dead, she had merely suffered a necessary reduction. He sensed the edgy crackle of her thoughts, like the intermittent popping of a fire gone to embers.

"It's okay, baby. It's okay." He put an arm under her back and lifted her, supporting her about the waist. Then he hauled her over to the sofa. He helped her to sit, and sat beside her, an arm about her shoulders. Her head lolled heavily against his, the softness of her breast pressed into his arm. He could hear the music coming from her, along with the electric wrack and tumble of her thoughts. They had never been closer than they were right now, he thought. Like a couple of high school kids on a couch date. Leaning together, hearing the same music, hearts still, minds tuned to the same wavelength.

He wanted to say something, to tell her how much he loved her, but found that he could no longer speak, his throat muscles slack and useless.

Well, that was okay.

Rachel knew how he felt, anyway.

But if he could speak, he'd tell her that he'd always known they could work things out, that though they'd had their problems, they were made for each other...

Hey, Wilma, he'd say, yabba dabba doo.

And then they would begin to explore this new and calmer life, this purity of music and brightness.

A little too much brightness, if you asked him.

The light was growing incandescent, as if having your life ultimately simplified admitted you to a dimension of blazing whiteness. It was streaming up from everything, from the radio, the television, from Rachel's parted lips, from every surface, whitening the air, the night, whiting out hope, truth, beauty, sadness, joy, leaving room for nothing except the music, which was swelling in volume, stifling thought, becoming a kind of thirsting presence inside him. It was sort of too bad, he said to himself, that things had to be like this, that they couldn't have made it in the usual way, but then he guessed it was all for the best, that this way at least there was no chance of screwing anything up.

Jesus, the goddamn light was killing his eyes!

Might have known, he thought, there'd be some fly in the ointment, that perfection didn't measure up to its rep.

He held onto Rachel tightly, whispering endearments, saying, "Baby, it'll be okay in a minute, just lie back, just take it easy," trying to reassure her, to help her through this part of things. He could tell the light was bothering her as well by the way she buried her face in the crook of his neck.

If this shit kept up, he thought, he was going to have to buy them both some sunglasses.